Lyrics of an Angel
poetry in reality

Also by
AMANI ABDUL

Lions Lair

MUSE: The Lyrics

**Chasing Peace: Freeing Your Spirit and
Releasing Your Soul**

MUSE Poetry CD
www.AmaniAbdul.com
Amazon.com
iTunes
CDBaby

Lyrics of an Angel
poetry in reality

by Amani Abdul

All rights reserved.
No part of this publication may be transmitted, stored in a retrieval system, reproduced, copied, scanned, recorded, distributed or otherwise, in any printed or electronic form whatsoever without the prior written permission of the author. Please do not participate in or encourage piracy of copyrighted materials in violation of the author's rights. Purchase only authorized editions.

Original Copyright © 1999
by Amani Abdul

Revised Copyright © 2012
by Amani Abdul

ISBN 978-1-929985-07-4

Cover design by Frankie Fultz

For orders or information, write to:
info@AmaniAbdul.com

www.AmaniAbdul.com

Angel Heart Publishing

As i sit and play
life's everyday game,
i break free
to redeem my name.

Poetry is a form of expression
and the expressions in this book
reveal what I have seen, heard, tasted,
felt, and encountered at a crucial
turning point in my life.
This book comes to you straight
from my soul. It is written from a world
that I have witnessed, a world that I
wanted to share with you. I'm sure as you
read though the pages, you will feel me--
no matter what your world is like...

ACKNOWLEDGEMENTS

I thank God and the Universe for blessing me with such an incredible talent; and am very grateful to have such a wonderful family and fabulous friends who continue to support me and encourage me to practice my craft.

Gus aka Goose, Ray, Dee Dee, Nickie, Ken, and My Dear Michael (R.I.P), I love you all…here's to those good times, bad times, and everything in between. Thank you for ALWAYS having my back.

Much Love to Frankie Fultz, aka My Martian, for his out of this world artistic talents and direction.

*Dedicated to my heartbeat and greatest accomplishment, my son,
Ameer.
I love YOU more than I can ever describe, and more than you could ever imagine. It is because of you that I chose to seek the light verses to live in darkness.*

*And to all the children of the world, for they are the precious jewels
of today and the bright minds of tomorrow- Love, Treasure, Nurture, and Treat Them Right.*

A Note from the Author

I have written many poems and have been writing for as long as I can remember. Writing has always provided me the outlet I needed to release my thoughts and emotions. These are some of my earlier poems- they were written between the ages of eighteen and twenty-four. During this transitional period in my life, I was going through a mental, emotional and spiritual struggle, even more so than during the years of my youth. During these years, I came to know what true friendship, unconditional love, spiritual warfare and transitional testing were all about. To this very day, when I read these words, they still sting my heart and bring waves of tears to my eyes…just to think that I used to hurt so bad and managed to get through it is flabbergasting to me at times. Always remember that your current reality is never fixed and God's grace is infinite.

When I assess my life, I think about where I've come from (my foundation), where I've been (tests and lessons), where I am (tunnel of life), and where I'm headed (my purpose). I conclude that all of these different periods in my life, these different spheres were all conjured up to allow me the best experiences in order for me to evolve into the spiritual being I am destined to be.

Your situations and experiences don't define you, what you learn from them and how you apply the knowledge from those situations and experiences in your future lessons and tests defines you.

With that said, I bring to you my first book of poetry. I truly hope you enjoy the lyrical ride, as life is an amazing journey… hold on tight…and make sure you smile through the bumps.

Lyrics

Through My Big Brown Eyes

the future
ameer
my heart goes out to you
through my big brown eyes
has death found you? ask yourself
the dope man rhyme
what is a friend?
masquerade
the bottle goes around
provocative flower
the bouquet
see what you hear
spring

Deep Within Me

before i go to sleep
don't paint me a picture
deep within me
beauty is deep
bare essentials
precious
joy and pain
what is pain?
foretold fortune
love me
forgive me
a prayer to God
brighter tomorrows

Love Hangover

oh, how nice it would be
i do appreciate you
love hangover
strike out
my problem
love is a lie
a heart so deep
bye bye love
why can't i get over you?
the rose
silly rabbit

Heaven Calls
my best friend (i miss you)
I'm sorry
memories of Jadda
a heavenly blessing
thinking back
sold gold
thank you for being you

Encore
the ones

Through My Big Brown Eyes

THE FUTURE

As we continue to strive
let us keep all hope alive
for our children to survive
the great tests of the past
these are moments to treasure
times to make last

For us to create a new future today
let us sit down, think and pray
let us all try to instill
knowledge into these children
we need to fill

Tap into their inner most thoughts
tell them that taking an easy way out
has its cost
it's okay to be anxious
it's okay to want the best
but ask them if they want to
end up just like the rest

For a brighter future will come
from the knowledge within
but you must let them know
that it's okay to make mistakes
we all live to sin

They must strive for what they want
go all the way
be all they can be
but only knowledge will set you free

STOP
LOOK
and LISTEN
to all that's around
TURN
to SEE
and HEAR
to the crying for help sound

It might not be obvious
it might not be in your face
but you can bet your life
it's going down in the same place

You don't have to be a genius
although that would be nice
but you can't make a life
out of a snake-eyes game of dice

Just try your best to do what you can
and you'll be amazed on how that will
make you a better woman or man

The future is yours if you want it to be
just reach out and grab
that never ending mind key.

AMEER

It's 8 o'clock
as I lie here
I wonder…
What's about to go down???
I thought I was going crazy with
anticipation
never thought that I'd have something
that I could later crown

Two and a half hours go by
and still nothing yet
I tell my mom to leave
"I'll be okay" I say
she needed her rest
I couldn't have let her stay

A couple of hours later
and here I am
speechless and in pain
I thought I'd be okay
that was kinda lame

A few more hours go by
and by now
my pain has turned to torture
I felt tears at my eyes
it's now 6 in the mornin'
and everyone could hear my early cries

These people keep coming and going
to make sure I'm alright

I have to make a call
to tell mom I'm uptight

I asked her to come back
I needed her at my side
the pain was getting worse
and I could no longer subside

More hours go by
and still nothing
a lady comes by with a piece of paper
saying something..
"You might have to sign this ma'am
we might have to take you in."
God has answered my prayers
I'll do anything
to stop this pain from within

More time goes by
I feel like I'ma die
and the lady comes back to say..
"Honey sign on the dotted line,
lay back close your eyes,
everything will be okay."

My mom got scared
she walked out of the room
I asked her to stay
told her everything will be alright real
soon

They moved me somewhere
with big bright lights

and silver sharp things
my stomach tightened
I felt it cringe

They put me on another bed
strapped my arms down
and put something over my head
.
.
.
.
.

What's going on
I feel real weak
can hardly see my mom
nor can barely speak

but…
what is that I hear
a crying voice
I named him ***"Ameer"***
because he's the prince of *My Choice*.

MY HEART GOES OUT TO YOU
(Dedicated to Children of Child Abuse)

i see the children of today
outside as they happily play
without any worries or any doubts
but there's always one
who strays about

that child there
my heart goes out to
and out of a bundle
there are those few

who keep their pain
bottled up inside
they cry to their self
and try to hide

they're miserable and feel deceived
by those whom they were by conceived

they feel abandoned
they feel alone
they just can't call that house a home
they're feeling confused, scared and
betrayed
by those who they thought really cared

but to those who
my heart goes out to
i want you to know
that there are those who will help you

scream if you wish
or simply extend out your hand
and i'll do my best
to be there and to stand
beside you
and help you overcome that terrible
tragedy
that to your life has come to be

so cheer up dear children
there are friends out there that you've got
and no one will ask you for anything
or against you plot

we just want for you your happiness
because misery is nothing to live for
i just want you to see sunshine
throughout every closed door

THROUGH MY BIG BROWN EYES

Trough My Big Brown Eyes
is a land of enormous size
of all different colors
and created dyes
yet some who think they're supreme
think they're the prize
so I guess that gives them
the right to patronize
when are we all going to realize
GOD created man
of different colors, shapes and size
so don't judge me
'cause one day I will arise
and just might look down on you
Through My Big Brown Eyes.

HAS DEATH FOUND YOU?
Ask Yourself

For those who want to live the glamorous life…

Ask Yourself
Is it worth the stab of a knife?

Ask Yourself
Is it worth the shot of a gun?
and across the street there's someone
saying that your life is done

Ask Yourself
Is it worth for your mama to cry?
as she watches her beloved on the
sidewalk lie
drenched in a puddle the color red
just because her child has been misled

Ask Yourself
Is it worth the pain your friends will carry?
holding on to your casket that they now
will bury

Ask Yourself
Is it worth the nightmares your mate will
have?
of the days you both sat back and laughed

and until you've thought about
all of the above

the ones around you
and the ones you love
and still choose this path to go through

don't look back

but

Death
Has
Found
You!

THE DOPE MAN RHYME

dope man, dope man
deep as you might be
dope man, dope man
you've got to set yourself free

dope man, dope man
so you think you're a star
dope man, dope man
you'll never get far

dope man, dope man
it's a real shame
dope man, dope man
only two ways out of this game

dope man, dope man
it's a tragedy
dope man, dope man
how your life will end up to be

WHAT IS A FRIEND?

What is a friend?
a friend is a person who'll be there
for you until the very end

if you need a shoulder
a friend is always there
if you have a true friend
you'll never ask yourself if anyone cares

a friend will cheer you up
when you are down
a friend will make you smile
instead of frown

a friend is always there
to lend a helping hand
when you feel as if you've had enough
and can barely stand

a friend is always there for you
whenever you're in doubt
that friend is always there
forever to bail you out

a friend will always tell you
when you're wrong
that friend will always be there for you
to keep you strong

a friend is someone you can talk to

about each and everything
that friend won't ever desert you
and will always be your right wing

a friend is supportive
and believes in you all the way
that friend is always there
forever and everyday

a friend will never leave you
when you're feeling down and low
that friend won't ever deceive you
that friend will never go

So What is a Friend?
a friend is always behind you
in whatever you may do
that friend is always there for you
forever honest and true.

— *Cut* —

Note: In this life we encounter many people that come in and out of our lives for various reasons and at different seasons. Some people, I like to call them "fillers" we let in ourselves but everyone has an agenda to fulfill in our life and no one is promised to stay.

Whatever the situation, there will be an outcome- some good, some bad, some just plain ugly. So remember to choose your Friends wisely.

The next time you call someone your
Friend, think about this poem and ask
yourself if they are worthy of this title;
because a lot of the time, they are not.

MASQUERADE

What is it about me
that you hate so?
Is it the radiance
of my everlasting glow?
Why is it that
you don't care for me much?
Is it 'cause men find
the end of my fingertips
an enticing touch?
Why must you down me?
Why be so cruel?
Is it for the sake to hear
someone tell you
what you said was cool?
True I wear the finest of threads
money can buy,
and eat the best of breads
mostly I like rye,
I can have any man
dance on my bed and try,
but that doesn't excuse
your very fictitious lie.

Don't get me wrong
you haven't stopped me at all
I just go through life
as a Masquerade ball.

What is it about me?
Why do you so despise?
Is it that I've got fire icicles

or gold diamonds in my eyes?
Is it my mouth so small,
yet a voice deep?
Is it my long black hair,
that you can get very cheap?
Is it my body,
such a perfect size?
Or my gentle little hand,
that will make any man arise?
So you sit there and ridicule me
with nothing but envy on your mind--
I just sit back and enjoy
the Masquerade that I've defined.
What is it about me
that you just can't stand?
Is it that I can have my choice
of each and every man?
Or is it my charisma
that you just can't touch?
Is that why you hate me
ever so much?

My smile brightens a room
as I walk through the door,
people turn and look
attention throughout the floor,
personality so real
sweet and kind,
always polite
never stuck up,
with a great intellectual mind.
At times I might not say much
I may even seem cold,

but that doesn't excuse you
for fabricating the stories
that have been told.

You think you know me
my boldness so cruel,
I've done nothing wrong
but play you for a fool.
Just because you
don't understand me,
just because you
don't have all the facts-
Is that why you make up
what your story lacks?

You say I'm wrong
for the things I've done and do,
I've only hurt the ones
who to me were untrue.
You can't bring one person
to say they know me,
truly at all,
that's why I go through life
as a Masqurade ball.

A heart half of cotton
and half of stone,
I've had few rights
and far more wrongs,
but that's what keeps me
keeps me strong,
going through this Masquerade
we've been playing for so long.

I can flip the script
at any given time,
I can flip a script
just like I create a rhyme,
you think you're hurting me
by dropping a silly dime,
you think you're hurting me
with your fictitious crime,
but I must tell you
I really don't have the time,
to let you stop me in my prime.
But if you really must have
your fun that way,
I will tell you
it's really okay,
cause I'ma keep on living
my life day to day,
and keep on creepin'
on such envious pray,
yet still
I enjoy this little game we play,
it's only done
in a MASQUERADE way.

THE BOTTLE GOES AROUND

round and round
the bottle goes
where it stops
one never knows
you sit around
a bunch of hoes
sippin' your troubles away
as the music blows
the bartender asks
"Are you okay?"
and you reply
"I would like another
one of those."
round and round
the bottle goes.

PROVOCATIVE FLOWER

luxury
hard not to stare
luster
of pure delicate care
erotic
&
exotic
enticing you into a psychotic dare
of lust and passionate desire
her luscious nature will set any anybody's
mind on fire

EXOTIC BOUQUET

I don't like my roses red
I don't care for violets blue
but a gift of an orchid
is a much felt true
I love them in violet
I prefer them in white
but if I can't get those
I'll take the exotic type

I love hibiscus
and calla lilies too
flowers always put a smile on my face
when I feeling down and blue

they're so sensual, a beauty rare
they stand out beyond compare

I like the way they feel
I love the way they smell
I admire their Godly design
crafted oh so well

what a creation
what a delight
these provocative exotic flowers
are such a gorgeous sight

SEE WHAT YOU HEAR

those who claim
to know me
know nothing
but what I
allowed them to see

for those who claimed
to have spoken to me
have heard nothing
but what they wanted it to be

and for those who claimed
to have sat, walked
and played with me
may not have done exactly so;
they just told a tale
that they thought
you'd be interested to know

SPRING

as i awake
early in the morning
to the sounds
of the sweet birds sing
i sense to myself
that it's a sure sign of spring
i raise the blinds
and open up the window
to look outside
and smell the fresh spring breeze blow
i see the green in the grass
that's starting to grow
i see the buds on the trees
beginning to show
so i hurry up
to get my early morning jog
out of the way, cause i want to hurry
and start planning out my day
i jump in the shower
dress in less than an hour
make my phone calls
to see what i have to do
i make my rounds
finish up early
and catch the sun
before it goes down
…man… already the day is through.

Deep Within Me

BEFORE I GO TO SLEEP

i lay awake every night in my bed
all these thoughts run through my head
I think about the what's
the where's
the when's
the why's
and the how's

always wondering
what am I to do now
I dream about
peace, love and laughter
that's the kind of life
I've always longed after
I've looked long and hard
but found nothing there
I just keep going through
this terrible despair

I've often wondered…
Why was this happening to me?
but you know what they say-
"What goes around, comes around,
and what will be, will be."

See, I've been true to few
yet crossed so many
that all I can do now
is get a pretty penny
but as far as life's pleasures
and life's love

I can't get those
until I'm forgiven above

So I cry myself to sleep every night
knowing tomorrow will be another fight
I know I'm strong enough
that I'll pull through
but nothing can explain my pain
and this feeling so blue

You see, I thought life was a gamble
and I gambled and lost
now it's me that's paying the cost
I thought love was a game
and I played to the end
but now it's my broken heart
that won't mend

I guess you can say
it doesn't pay to play
God knows I wish
someone told me that back in the day

So I'll have to sit back
and let this course take its toll
or until God decides
to take my soul

I know that I have made
many mistakes in the past
but that was a life
that wasn't meant to last

So I just lie here
in the darkest of sorrows
and hope that someday
I'll see brighter tomorrows

DON'T PAINT ME A PICTURE

don't paint me a picture
of how life could have been
don't paint me a picture
for here I lay alive in sin

don't paint me a picture
of how life could be
don't paint that pretty picture
because I can't see it in me

don't paint that perfect picture
for my mentality
don't paint me that picture
because I live in reality.

DEEP WITHIN ME

i won't let you see
deep within me
NO!
deep within me
i can't let you see
because if you see
deep within me
you'll find it
                A

lonely place to be

BEAUTY IS DEEP

Far beneath my surface
lays another person inside,
a person like no other
but yet the other presides.

They're two of one
but one is greater,
it's the go-getter in me
my renown debater.

It stays hidden deep
within my soul,
it takes a special key
for this part to unfold.

It's a different saga
that takes part,
down, deep, beneath
at my heart.

And there you stand
thinking you have me all figured out,
but then as you turn
you begin to doubt.

Quit trying to figure out
my true identity,
just take what you can
and appreciate my quality.

I have a lot to offer

that only in time you will see,
it takes a special person to realize
the inner beauty in me.

BARE ESSENTIALS

i see her standing there
almost bare
on a lighted runway
wondering, "What is she doing here?"
[she says] "All spotlights are focused upon me."
but for some reason
she always blacks out and can't see

as she stops to turn
I see her eyes burn
[and she says] "I wonder if they can see right through me?
I wonder if they know that I want to be free?"

I wonder to myself...
Do they know that she doesn't care
about those who are just sitting there?
Do they know that she can't be true
until she finds an alternative life view?

and I ask her...
What are you doing here?
as I turn and see
her reflection in the mirror
You don't belong in such a place
Why are you doing this?
[she drops her face]...

Sitting here listening

to a bunch of lines
from men in fine vines
a true friend in here
you will never find
there are very few
who are even honest and kind.

Guys ask her...
"Why do you look so mean?"
they just didn't understand the fact
that she didn't care too much for the
scene.

They thought she was stuck up
they thought she was riding high
they just didn't know that
she would go home every night and cry.

[she says] "Sure, the money's good
but I'd give it all up
if only I could."

but there she was
accustomed to certain things
except she didn't know
the freedom that joy, love
and peace could bring.

she felt stuck
trapped in a lifestyle
she couldn't afford
and was selling dope door to door.

So she subjected herself
to continue doing what she did
until the day she finally had the strength
to just up and quit.

PRECIOUS

There was a little girl
who lived in a shoe
she had so many problems
she didn't know what to do

Her parents were mean
and very cruel
but acted like as if she was
a precious jewel

They wouldn't let her leave the house
they wouldn't let her play
so the little girl decided
to run away

She met a man
as nice as can be
looks can be deceiving
trust me you'll see

He was her first love
and she loved him so
but she never knew
he was a hoe

This girl you see
was so naive
and to make it so bad
she was getting ready to conceive
This man played with her mind
and he broke her heart

now this young lady
had to make a new start

She met a man
she had met before
and said to herself
"Let's see what this one's got in store."

Although she loved this man
she hurt him so
and didn't feel the pain
'til he had to go

She stayed with this man
for a very long time
until the day
of that horrible crime

She went back to the other
they tried to work things out
for she still loved him
and there was no doubt

But this man was so insincere
when this girl tried to be so dear
and one day
when she looked in the mirror
everything became clear

You see the young lady just needed
some love and care
from a friend who would
always be there.

JOY AND PAIN

Here's a little story about Joy and Pain
I hardly knew Joy
but always ran into Pain
you see, Joy came and went kinda fast
but good ol' Pain always seemed to last
oh, what an awful spell it would cast
the affect it had was always mass
but I'd always tell myself that he would pass
that awful feeling of Pain so vast.

WHAT IS PAIN?

Pain is a feeling down deep inside
a feeling that you forever try and hide
but no matter what
it always comes to light
it's a feeling that you just can't fight
Pain is what you feel when
someone lets you down
tells you one thing
and does another as soon as you turn
around
Pain is felt when you find out
about a certain something that you knew
but yet kept in doubt

your feelings turn shades of blue
when you're hurt by someone you thought
you knew
a scar will always remain
of that feeling that they call Pain.

FORETOLD FORTUNE

I have always been told
that to have
is not always to hold
the story of your life
has already been foretold
no matter how you try
to hold it together
or to mold.

LOVE ME

Love Me
love me right
Love Me
even out of sight
Love Me
unconditionally
Love Me
mentally and emotionally
Love Me
for who I am or am not
Love Me
not for what I can offer or have got
love my heart
even though it is of stone
touch it
and see that it is alone
love my mind and all its wicked ways
see into it
and witness the games it plays
Love Me
love my rights
don't down my wrongs
just be there for me
sing me a happy song.

FORGIVE ME

Forgive Me
forgive all I've done
Forgive Me
forgive all I've become
understand me
understand the person I am
understand me
even though you might think
– I don't give a damn
see past my cold icy ways
let pass my vindictive days
see through
my inner mystery
see my pain and misery
just forgive me
you don't have to necessarily forget
notice everything I've done
has caused me regret
Forgive Me
just give me one more chance
Forgive Me
and let's start a new dance.

A PRAYER TO GOD

Oh dear God,
I send you this prayer
knowing that you are always there
you know I've been in a lot of pain
and it's all bottled up inside
deep in my consciousness
where it grows and hides
I cry and cry
but it never seems to help
you see I've realized I'm all by myself
alone and lonely
lonely and alone
out in this cold world on my own
I lie in this bed alone at night
with no one to trust
or hold tight
I just lie here and stare
at the ceiling above me
hoping to someday to find peace
and the one who truly loves me
sometimes I wish that I was dead
it beats lying here with these thoughts
running through my head

BRIGHTER TOMORROWS

here I sit thinking about tomorrow
trying to see if there is something there
past the sorrow
of this misery that has become of me
that took over my body so completely
I wish I had a way to set my mind free
of this feeling that took over me
so I sit here and dream of a better
tomorrow
with hopes of ending all my pain,
misery and sorrow

Love Hangover

OH, HOW NICE IT WOULD BE

oh, how nice it would be
if I can only find
the perfect mate for me
one that's a sure FINE date
who's hardly ever late
he'd be SWEET and KIND
with a great INTELLECTUAL mind
who's TALL and HANDSOME
and sure has some
CHARISMA with a SMILE
that just brings his face to a glow
hardly ever whines or moans
and every time I see him
my mouth just falls to the floor
a man whose BIG and STRONG
when I see him
I'll know
he's the prince I've been waiting for all
along
someone who turns me on with his
mysterious eyes
doesn't fabricate any lies
and can be my FRIEND through all and all
I can see us together hand in hand
and when we're out
we're sure to have a ball
life will be so grand
he'll make me feel…ooh so good
like only he could
we'll both be able to see
it will be so right

there will be no maybe's or might's
oh, how nice it would be.

I DO APPRECIATE YOU

I want you to know that I think of you
and appreciate all that you do
from our late night dinners
and our early morning talks
to our afternoon departures
and evening walks
our playfulness
and the common things we like to do
all remind me of why I fell in love with
you
so don't think for a minute
I've forgotten what you do
I appreciate everything you've done
and will always love you!!

PS thanks for the flowers, breakfast, and
the rose on my nose. Love you.

LOVE HANGOVER

ACHING
BREAKING
what used to be breath taking
GONE
like a winters day dawn
WET CHEEKS
HEART REEKS
of what used to be so sweet
EYES STING
VOICES RING
no longer those warm nights of spring

STRIKE OUT

a far away blow
a gentle touch
a wet one on the lips
is a bit too much…Strike 1

I feel you coming on
a tad strong
hey baby, what's the rush?
what's your angle?
what's your point?
you ask me if I would
mind going back to
your joint…Strike 2

what's up hon?
where are you coming from?
you tell me one thing
and now you're marching
to the beat of a different drum… Strike 3

I understand
I've been in this position before
you're just another one
of those who just wants to
score…Strike Out!

MY PROBLEM

I have a problem I would like to share
this problem of mine that's causing my
despair
you see My Problem is love
and it hurts so much
but yet I still go back
for that inviting touch
see this love of mine
has got me feeling so blue
I wish I had my friend
to clue in on what to do
day to day, I feel my heart turning cold
and I never want to hate
the one I love to hold
I see this change coming about
sometimes I think it's here
but I fight it and doubt
I've had this feeling before
of being so bold
but that's another tale to be told
some say to leave this love of mine
they say that he's no good
I try to explain and wish they understood
I tell them that this love of mine
is really too deep to leave
and that stuff they're preaching
I just didn't seem to want to believe
if they were in my shoes
Would they not do the same?
save that so called love knowledge
it's too lame for the love game

people always want to say
what they would do if they were you
don't believe that crap
'cause it isn't true
I speak for my friends
because I tried to be that friend before
who tried to settle someone else's score
didn't believe that I was the one that was blamed
for her man hitting on me
what a shame
so this I will deal with on my own
or I won't forgive myself for leaving him alone
I'll deal with my problem until the bitter end
because once it's over, it will be OVER
and this relationship will no longer mend
either way it goes, I won't say I didn't give it my all
at the end, it will be his regret and his fall.

LOVE IS A LIE

in my eyes I had visions of you
caring, sharing and always willing to be
there

as my tears start falling, sadness appears
and I quickly realize that you never truly
cared

so here I am facing reality
on how dear and true I've been with you
as I toss and turn through the night
wondering where you are and with who
wondering does she love you as much as I
do?

you tell me that you've done nothing
that I'm the one for you

I listen to your diluted reality
and question if what you say is true

I called your house
someone answered the phone
said you weren't home
I call back
she answers again
come to find out
she was your fling

you can't lie about this one
'cause this is just too low

this isn't working out
and I will have to let you go

no need to turn back now, I'm gone
this time you were definitely in the wrong

Love Is A Lie
be careful of what you do
never take a man's word
even if he tells you he's true.

A HEART SO DEEP

I lie here staring into the starry sky
thinking about your very deceitful lies
here we are talking about spending our
lives together
and I find out that you're out wooing
others
you kept telling me that our love was true
you want to be with me
and I wanted to be with you
but when reality hit
I finally realized then
that you're not the man
I loved within
so I came to the conclusion
that you're one less person for me to know
and with this said, I must pack up and go
A Heart So Deep
never realizes the truth
you were *there* for me
while I was *here* for you.

BYE BYE LOVE

bye bye love
I've had just about enough
it was real while it lasted
but you ain't nothin' but a bastard
a typical hoe
you understand the type, I know
I can't say I wish you luck
honey, when it comes to you,
I really don't give a &^@%!

bye bye love
putting up with your crap
only made me tough
thank you for this lesson
too bad knowing you
wasn't a blessin'
I'll see you around, I'm sure
doin' what you do best
you ain't nothin' but a male whore
a man, you are not
a chicks instinct is what you got
runnin' around playing silly mind games
messin' around with all kinds of dames
lies, games and lines
I should have known, baby
you were never mine
sorry and confused is what you are
growing up for you is much too far
runnin' the streets
thinkin' about nothin' but money
and the next dame that you knock up

will be your honey
for the night, or maybe even day
but listen up babe someday you'll pay
our relationship was one big lie
and all I have to say now is
BYE BYE!

WHY CAN'T I GET OVER YOU?

Why can't I get over you my mystical rose?
spin the bottle
one never knows
Why can't I get over you like the rest of those?
Why can't get over you?

Why can't I get over you the one that I adore?
every time I see you
I only want more
Why can't I get over you like the ones before?
Why can't I get over you?

Why can't I get over those memories of you?
I strain my brain to think
but haven't the slightest clue
Why can't I get over the things that you do?
Why can't I get over you?

Why can't I get over your strange sensation that I can't find?
and every time I see you
you keep that same ol' line
Why can't I get you straight off my mind?
Why can't I get over you?

THE ROSE

I remember the first time I saw the rose
I wanted to touch it but I just froze
I was enchanted with the mystical touch
the rose bestowed upon me
but even then I knew it would be too much
so I just sat back and admired from afar
the special rose that everyone thought was
such a star
until one day it was sent over to me
so careless, open, wild and free
I wanted to help it flourish
I wanted to help it grow
what can I say,
I wanted to take care of it so
but instead it fell apart
right in front of me
and I knew then
that taking it in wouldn't be so smart
so I just went with the flow
and let the little carefree rose go…

SILLY RABBIT

you say you miss me
but when you kiss me
i feel your intenseness
uplifts me
i don't know what
you came here for
but please
don't mistake me for a whore
i need a man to love and adore
you just want to use and abuse
and if I let ya
you'll come back and reuse
but the trick to the plan
is to find out
if you're a real, true man
and if you're not
i'll throw you out in the can
with the rest of your kind and clan
but first i'll use and abuse ya
tell ya that i miss ya
and since your ego is on high
i'll come back and reuse ya
and you don't ask why
cause you think you're fly
but guess what
you got got silly guy
now you don't understand
all of a sudden
i stopped calling
ruined your whole plan

When Heaven Calls

MY BEST FRIEND - I MISS YOU
(In Loving Memory of My Dear Michael)

My best friend - I see your smile
down that long and endless mile
I hear your laughter - in the life after
You shared your joys of love - now you're up above
in a world so unknown - as I sit here all alone
I wonder what you're doing day to day
I know I can't join you
but I will definitely pray
for you to be resting in peace
looking down at us and smiling with ease
only God knows
that I miss you with all my heart
and it's just too bad
that we have to be apart
I wish the best for you
and pray for you every night
may you be okay - may you be alright
I could be anywhere
and would think of you
and cry when I think about
just how much I miss you.

I will love you…always and forever…

I'M SORRY

It's clearly too late for I'm Sorry but here it goes...
I'm Sorry for the things I've done
I know I've hurt you worse than that loaded gun
I don't know what I was thinking about back then
hanging around with those women and men
I know I let you down many a time
and treated you as if you weren't worth more than a dime
but whenever I needed you
You always made sure I was on the right track
and all I did was put another knife to your back
I repeat I'm Sorry for everything I've done
I know I've hurt you more than anyone
I know you trusted me with your life
And all I did was continue to stab you with my invisible knife.
PLEASE FORGIVE ME
PLEASE HEAR MY PLEA
I regret everything I've done
and my heart is in constant agony
I promise to never hurt another that loves me ever again
I wish I had a chance to say this to you in person, my friend

truly I'm Sorry from the bottom of my heart
it's too bad I've awakened when we had to part.

MEMORIES OF JIDDA
(In Loving Memory of My Jidda Amoun)

I remember sitting next to her
as she combed her long, silky, black hair
it always shined in the sun
reflected by the mirror
that she sat in front of
this lady that I dearly love.

Her skin stayed a pretty bright glow
and her step was nothin' short of a pure
flow.
Her voice was so gentle
but if you made her mad
she got temperamental.

However, to me
she was always so sweet
and I'll never forget
when she made my favorite treat.

I remember when I was about 3 or 4
and would ask this lady
that I admired and adored
all these questions that I thought of
and she would answer me
Honestly and with Love.

Her warm and loving smile
I still see before me
as I sit in this denial
and wish this wasn't to be.

I haven't seen this lady in so many years
and now I'm writing this poem
with falling tears.
I want her to know
I love her with all my heart
and may she forgive me for being absent
and us being apart.

I'll never forget
my first few years of life and happiness
that I spent with this lady
who had so much courage,
strength, class, pride and finesse.

So now I just sit here
in this Twilight Zone
and keep remembering my
Dear, Sweet, Jidda Amoun
and God please let my Jidda know
that her little Amani will always love her
so
and God please tell my Jidda up above
that in Amani's heart, she will always be
Cherished, Remembered, Treasured and
LOVED.

*Jidda (Arabic): Grandma

A HEAVENLY BLESSING
(My Condolences to the Joyce Family in Beloved Memory of Claxton Joyce)

Oh Heavenly Father up above
bless thy soul with eternal love
bless he who was good to all
bless he who has got his call
may he have a heavenly sleep
let thy know
his memories
we will forever keep
bless his family
whom he treasured so much
bless them all
with your gentle touch
bless thou who was sweet and kind
bless he who is in our hearts and minds
may he look down on us from up above
and laugh at the spread of love
that he passed while he was here
please let thy know
that he is still
LOVED,
close and dear.

Rest in Peace Mr. Joyce.

THINKING BACK

I know You see my misery
of suffering pain
and the tears I cry
as if it were rain.

You're the only one who understood
what I was going through
and pretended as if You never knew
of all my troubles
as they constantly grew
You acted as if they were few

When I needed a shoulder
You were always there
now I just sit around and compare.

I always think and dream
of what could have been
of all the joys and pains
we shared back then.

Now I sit back and think
about how lonely life has become
and I can't help but wonder…
Will this happiness of mine ever come?

I remember the talks we used to share
and now I feel as if there's no one there…
You were my friend
yes one of many
but You were the best

and now I haven't any.

You taught me a lot
about life and its wonders
and now look at me
I just keep going under.

No matter what I did
and how I did it
You were always there
to help me deal with it.

You always told me that I could do
whatever I wanted to do
and whatever it was
I'd be a success at it too.

You always taught me to take charge
and think clear
and before I knew it
a new life would appear.

I must say You taught me well
it's just too bad
You left me alone
in this life of hell.

SOLD GOLD
(Dedicated in Loving Memory of R.C. and to all my friends that are no longer here)

my friends who thought their bodies
were made of gold
who lived a life isolated and cold
whose smiles were worth billions
whose estates averaged out to millions
those who walked around
in alligator shoes and minks
twenty-five hundred dollar suits
and solid gold links
who thought that they were the ultimate
ones
and later died from bullets of guns

I wish you listened when you were around
now you are six feet underground
I miss you all ever so dearly
you couldn't understand not even barely
of how different life has become for me
because I can't forget you all so easily
I pray for you all every night
I know someday that we will reunite
but for now I'll keep your spirits
with me wherever I may go
but there is one thing that I would
like for you all to know...

our memories
will forever be treasured

and our friendship
will never be measured

those who thought that they were bold
who lived a life isolated and cold
who thought their bodies
were bullet proof
and that they were made of gold
now their lives were being sold

May You ALL
Rest In Peace
and may this madness
DECREASE!!!

THANK YOU FOR BEING YOU
(Dedicated in Loving Memory of
Billy Dee)

You came into my life
with that dazzling smile
and jazzy style
that brightened my life
and reminded me to smile
with your crazy talk
and sexy walk
rolling thru that red carpeted isle
you picked my spirits up
as I was down
made me smile
instead of frown
those are just some of the memories
I have of you
always that friend
pulling me through
you were a great friend to me
and a real man too
I truly miss you
and the crazy things we used to do
Rest in peace, Billy Dee.

Encore

Last but not least, to the other folks in my life, the friends or associates I left out or the so called friends and associates I choose not to remember, here's a little something just for you:

THE ONES

For the ones who are here
and those who no longer are,
the ones who have stayed close
and the ones who have gone far.

The ones who never believed in me
or my abilities in any way,
and the ones who stabbed me
as soon as I looked away.

The ones who hid their snaky ways
shedding skin through the days…
The ones who threw away years
of smiles and tears
on nothing but pure trash;
when things got tight
certain ones were ready to dash.

The ones who speak of me
as if they really knew,
the rumors they put out
I have to come undo.

The ones who smile in my face
and my rep they try to disgrace.
The ones who are as fake as one could be
and hide behind a mask so you can't see--
that's right
the PhD'n,
rumor makin',
jealousy bein'

but will tell you all 'bout me an'
look me straight in the eyes
please STOP spreading the lies,
STOP the fakeness and alibis!
Because if you really knew me
in any sort of way,
you wouldn't have anything bad
to say or do
so screw you!

And if you ever at any point
called yourself getting next to me,
with friends like you all
who needs enemies…
PEACE.

(finally.)

*Thank you for allowing me to share some
of my life and work with you.
Much Love,*

~Amani Abdul

www.ingramcontent.com/pod-product-compliance
Lightning Source LLC
Chambersburg PA
CBHW071323040426
42444CB00009B/2068